A Horse Named Duke

by
Georgann S. Koenig

Edited by Douglas Early

AuthorHouse™
1663 Liberty Drive
Bloomington, IN 47403
www.authorhouse.com
Phone: 833-262-8899

This book is printed on acid-free paper.

ISBN: 978-1-4259-4104-8 (sc)
ISBN: 978-1-4634-8166-7 (e)

Print information available on the last page.

Published by AuthorHouse 11/11/2022

author HOUSE®

Krista likes to visit her grandfather, Rancher Chuck, at his ranch high in the mountains, far from the dust and noise of the nearest town. She likes being surrounded by tall trees, blue sky, and lots of ranch animals. There are chickens, pigs, geese, and a big herd of...

...horses!

Of all the ranch animals, Krista's favorite is a horse named Duke. Duke is a great big horse, a dark Appaloosa, brown with white spots all over his back.

One cool, crisp, spring morning, Krista woke when she heard Duke neighing. "Well, Duke," she heard Rancher Chuck say, "you look like you're feeling frisky today!" She looked out the window and saw Duke running around the pasture, kicking up his heels.

Krista dressed hurriedly and ran outside to the pasture gate. "Pop Pop," she said, "can we take Duke out for a ride today?"

"There's nothing I'd like better, but I don't know…," said Chuck. "Today I have to go the store to buy feed for the chickens, pigs, and geese. Then I have to unload the feed and put it in the hay barn. Then I have to make us some lunch, and after lunch I have to feed the animals and mend this gate. I have a full day of chores to do. I don't know if there'll be time enough to go riding too."

Krista looked crestfallen.

She thought for a moment and said, "What if I help? Could we get the chores done in time to go riding?"

"We might," Chuck said. "I tell you what. If you help, and if there's enough daylight left when we're done, I promise I'll saddle up Duke, and the three of us will go for a nice long ride."

So after breakfast, Krista and Chuck emptied the back of the truck so they could drive into town to buy feed.

At the feed store,

Chuck picked out the feed,

Krista looked at the shiny new horse tack,

Chuck helped the storekeeper to load the truck,

and Krista tried sitting in a big western saddle.

When they got back to the ranch, Chuck said, "Now your job is to feed the chickens, pigs, and geese,"

"Don't the horses need feed too?" asked Krista.

"No, there's plenty of fresh spring grass in the pasture for the horses to eat."

So Krista filled each of the feed bins, just as she had seen Chuck do. She was careful to close and latch the door of each animal pen when she was done. Meanwhile, Chuck unloaded the heavy feed sacks and stacked them in the hay barn.

By then, Krista and Chuck were tired and hungry, so they went into the ranch house to eat lunch.

After lunch, they felt sleepy. So Chuck sat in his favorite chair, Krista curled up on the sofa, and before long, both were sound asleep.

Krista woke when she heard the deep *honking* of geese and a frantic flapping of wings. She tiptoed past Chuck and slipped outside, being careful not to let the screen door slam shut.

What she saw amazed her. Excited geese were running madly around the yard. Oh, no! she thought, The geese have escaped from their pen! She ran after the geese to round them up.

Finally, she got the last goose back in its pen. She was latching the pen door when she noticed that the geese's feed bin was turned over. She wondered, Now how did that get turned upside-down?

As Krista started back to the house, she heard the shrill *squealing* of pigs. Pigs were running everywhere! The gate to the pigs' pen was wide open. She hurried to round up the pigs.

She was almost out of breath when she put the last pig back in its pen. As she was latching the gate, she saw that the pigs' feed bin was turned over. Scratching her head, she thought, Who let the pigs out? Who knocked over their feed? Is Pop Pop playing a trick on me?

All of a sudden, Krista heard the loud *clucking* of chickens. Looking up, she saw chickens fluttering, flapping, and flopping around the yard. "Here we go again!" she said, though no one but the animals could hear her.

When she had rounded up all the chickens and had firmly latched the chicken coop door, she noticed that the chicken feeder had been turned over. She thought, This is getting more and more mysterious. Who would have—no, who *could* have done this?

ഐൠ
19

She began to look for clues. The first thing she saw was hoof prints on the ground. Looking closer, she saw that they were horse hoof prints—BIG horse hoof prints!

The trail of hoof prints led from the *honking* geese's pen, past the *squealing* pigs' pen, and farther still to the *clucking* chickens' coop.

Suddenly, Krista heard a loud *stomping* sound. What could be making such a noise? She moved slowly toward the sound. It was coming from inside the hay barn.

She opened the barn door and peeked inside.

There, in the corner of the barn where Chuck kept Duke's saddle, stood great big Duke! At the sight of Krista, Duke gave a shrill *nicker*.

"Duke!" Krista said, "It was you! You opened the pens. You knocked over the feeders."

Rancher Chuck walked up—he had slept through everything! "What a mess!" he said. "The feed is scattered all over the ground."

Krista told him all about what had happened.

"Well, Duke," Chuck said, "I guess you broke through that old pasture gate. But why did you knock over the feeders? I'll have to take you back to the pasture, mend that gate, then clean up the pens…"

"Pop Pop," Krista said, "I know why Duke upset the bins. He doesn't want us to do chores. He wants us to go for a ride, just like I do."

Chuck looked at Krista, then Duke. Then he scratched his chin, shook his head, and laughed.

"You know, maybe Duke has a point," he said. "After all, a promise is a promise." So he saddled Duke, and the three of them went for a nice long ride along the trail to the lake.

When they got back, Krista and Chuck hosed off Duke and took him back to the pasture. Krista swept up the spilled feed, and Chuck mended the pasture gate.

As the sun set, they walked together back to the house. They laughed, and both of them said...

⚬⚬⚬

"What a horse!"

Printed in the United States
by Baker & Taylor Publisher Services